The Panini Lovers Co

by Rachel Hende

Acknowledgements

With grateful thanks to Michelle Newbold for inspiring me and providing some recipes of her own. Also thanks to my husband, who tried out the recipes and gave me lots of ideas.

Introduction

This book is aimed at anyone who has a panini press or sandwich maker. There are many different designs and models of these machines, but this book assumes that you have a machine which is a heavy press design and has flat plates. Some do come with grooves, lines or whatever and although the recipes may still work, they may need to be adapted slightly.

Paninis are growing in popularity but often people still make the same one over and over again and although it is nice to have an 'old favourite' it is also good to try something new. There could be an even better option that you have not tries. Others use their panini press a few times and then store it in the cupboard, because they are not inspired. Hopefully the idea and recipes here will help you to become more adventurous and get a lot of pleasure from your panini press, maybe it will never be put away in the cupboard again!

What is a Panini?

A panini is an Italian sandwich which grew in popularity in the 1980's when fast food became more common. It was very cool for young people to hang out at sandwich bars and the trend spread to America and then to other countries as well. The Italian panini is any type of sandwich, served hot or cold usually made from a thick roll and often filled with ham and cheese. In the UK and America they tend to be made from ciabatta bread and are always served hot. These days we tend to see them in coffee shops and they have a variety of fillings including vegetarian ones. Many people enjoy them and think that they cannot make them at home. In fact, it is perfectly possible to make them at home and even make them even better than the shops do!

Cleaning and Care of Panini Presses

If you have your own panini press, then it is very important to look after it properly. Read all of the care instructions on the box or leaflet that comes with it and make sure that you follow everything they recommend. The non-stick plates are very delicate and if they get scratched it will mean that all of the food cooked on them will stick. This is why it is very important to use silicone, plastic or wooden tools. You should really only need a fish slice to gently lift the sandwich off the plate anyway. The outside and inside can be cleaned with a soft cloth which has been dipped in soapy water and then rinsed off with a cloth rinsed in fresh water. The cloth should not be at all abrasive. It is important to wait until the press is cool before cleaning.

Types of Bread to Use

As mentioned before, it is traditional to use a ciabatta bread with the panini press and it certainly works well. However, there really is no rule as to which bread you should use. You may find that certain flavours work better with the fillings that you have chosen. It is fun to try different breads to see how it works and you can even just use sliced bread. It is worth bearing in mind that a thinner bread may not hold the filling as well and so you could risk that it will fall out of the sandwich on to the hot plate. This will not be a disaster but may make the plate more difficult to clean.

What Foods to Cook?

Many people restrict their cooking to just sandwiches. However, if you have a large flat plated panini press, then you can cook all sorts of things on it. You may find that the instructions that come with it, will give you some ideas and there are some recipes here where other products are cooked that are not sandwiches. Many people just think about cooking paninis and sandwiches on their panini press but the hot plates are suitable for cooking all sorts of things and so do not be close minded with regards to the opportunities.

Sandwich Fillings

Many people tend to stick to the same old sandwich fillings. They might go to their favourite coffee shop and always pick up the same one or use the same old fillings at home because that is what they have in the fridge. However, we are all being told that we should have a varied diet and by trying something new, we may even discover a fantastic new dish that we will cook for ourselves regularly. Often you can find a good staple ingredient and then add a variety of different things to it, until you find the perfect combination. It is great fun experimenting with the things that you have in the fridge to see what tastes good. It is also great to use different flavourings as well as trying sweet ingredients as well as savoury. Have fun with it, try some of the recipes here and try your own experiments. Hopefully reading the book will inspire you to try all sorts of creations!

Making Flavoured Oils

All paninis need some moisture or else they can be very dry and sometimes even quite hard to eat. Often they have cheese in and juicy vegetables but an alternative to this is to use a flavoured oil. The oil will add flavour as well as moisture to the sandwich. You can buy flavoured oils but it is very easy to make them yourself. Just take a nice oil, such as extra virgin olive oil. Put some in a dish with the item you want to flavour it with. Ideas would be things like chilli, garlic, basil and rosemary. Leave them together for a day or so, just covered over in the fridge and the flavour will get in to the oil. The amount you use is up to you – depending on how much you think you will need. The more of the flavouring ingredient you use, the stringer the oil will be. It is fun to experiment with different things and different combinations of flavours.

Using Herbs

Herbs can lift any dish and they are a great compliment to many foods which are used in paninis. For example basil works very well with tomato, rosemary with roasted vegetables, thyme with cheese and oregano with tomato and cheese. Dried herbs and fresh herbs tend to have quite different flavours and therefore you will need to try both to see which you like the best. You will also find that you need less of a dried herb as it has a more intense flavour. You may have favourites already and so try combining them with different paninis and see how well it works.

Cooking Times

You will find that your panini press might come with some instructions on how long to cook the paninis for. However, if you experiment with different types of foods, different breads and even cook from frozen, then the cooking times may change. It is usual that a panini roll or sandwich will take three minutes. If it is frozen it will probably take 30 seconds more. However, you may find that you prefer it crisper or less done and so you can try different times so that you get it to your liking. If you are not sure, then it is a good idea to keep checking it every 30 seconds to make sure that it does not burn. You will soon get used to knowing how long they take.

Tips

When you are cooking paninis then it is a good idea to experiment with different fillings. However, you will find that some fillings are better if they are cooked first. You can cook things on the actual panini press but it depends whether you want a chargrilled effect or a more thorough cooking. You will find that thin foods can cook through but other things may not.

When you are filling the panini then bear in mind that if you put sauce or chutney on both sides of the bread, it may stop any cheese you have inside from melting. It is therefore a good idea to make sure that you only put a pickle, chutney or relish on one piece of bread and have the cheese on another with other fillings in between. In some cases, very thick cheese may still not melt even if it is cooked on the edge for the full time, so it could be advisable to keep the slices thin.

If you are cooking something which is not a sandwich then bear in mind that the cooking time will be different to when you grill it. Because the item is being cooked from top and bottom you will only need to cook it for half the time. However, be sure to make sure it is piping hot throughout and check that it is not burning as it cooks.

Food to Serve with Panini

Paninis can often contain a lot of meat or cheese and so it can be nice to accompany them with some green leaves or salad. Of course, they can do perfectly well on their own but if you want to make them in to a meal, then it is nice to add a few more things to them.

If you do have a very high protein panini then it is also necessary to add a salad or some vegetables to make the meal more balanced. You may also like to have some mayonnaise, chutney or other sauce on the side of the plate for dipping the panini in to.

If you have cooked a sweet panini then you may like some yoghurt or cream to dip in to or even some sugar. Some fresh fruit, especially soft fruits would cut through the sweetness of most of the sweet paninis listed here.

Recipes

There are quite a few ingredients which can be used as a basic starter for a recipe and then a variation of this then used to make a dish. This means that some of the recipes could seem similar but they do each have their own unique flavour. Well some are recipes others are more ideas and just a case of putting ingredients together.

Paninis are very simple to cook but there is no reason why you should keep using the same fillings all of the time. Hopefully the recipes here will inspire you to make more exciting choices with regards to fillings and have fun experimenting yourself. Think about the foods you enjoy eating together and then have a go and see whether they work inside a panini. Most things do.

A panini can be a great way of using up left overs or just having a more exciting sandwich. They are great when you need something warm, but do not have the energy to cook or when you are on your own and just do not want to make a big meal.

They can be nutritious and do not have to be packed with calories, if you cook them right.

The recipes here are split in to sweet and savoury. Most people just think of paninis as savoury, but it is surprising how well they work with sweet fillings especially if you use a bread which has a sweeter taste.

Hopefully you will be inspired to try some new fillings and then go off and experiment by yourself.

Savoury Panini Recipes

Ham and Cheese Panini

Ham and cheese is a classic combination. It is a good idea to think carefully about the types of ham and cheese you are using. You do not want the flavour of one, to overpower the other. This means that if you

The Panini Lovers Cook Book by Rachel Henderson

are using a smoked ham, then you might want a strong cheese so that you can taste the cheese and the ham. However, you may wish the flavour of the ham to come through and therefore will want to use a mild cheese. It can be quite a balancing act which you might want to work out to perfect. However, it could be just a case of using up the ingredients in the fridge. You can also add additional flavourings to the sandwich such as mustard or chutney and you could also freshen it up with some herbs or rocket leaves.

Roasted Vegetables and Sun-Dried Tomato Paste

Roasted vegetables can be made out of any thing. A good combination could be onion, peppers and courgettes and you will need to cut them up very small and roast them in the oven with oil, until they are soft. You may like to add garlic and/or rosemary to add more flavour to them while they cook. It is great to make a big batch and then you can use them for successive days with a different combination of flavours. There are other recipes later which include vegetables that they could be used for.

This recipe is very simple and all you need to do is to spread both pieces of bread with sun-dried tomato paste. Then spoon a pile of vegetables on one slice, pop the other on the top and toast. Do not over fill the sandwich as the vegetables will fall out and may burn on the hot plate. This is a great vegan recipe – something which many people think is not possible with a panini. It is great served with avocado and lettuce salad.

Rocket, Mozzarella and Tomato

There is a slight technique with making this sandwich. If any rocket touches the hot plate then it will burn and so you need to make sure that it is all within the bread. It is best to put this on first and then the tomato. Use a nice big ripe tomato. Try to get one that is tasty, home grown would be best but also a vine ripened could be good. If you slice it thickly then it may not warm right through so decide how you want to do it. Then you need to sprinkle the mozzarella on top. You do not want to use too much

11

as it will melt and run out of the sandwich. Of course, you may enjoy having a bit of caramelised cheese along the edges of your sandwich.

Three Cheese

This is another sandwich where the cheese could run out of it. Combine the cheeses but do not use too much of each. Start off with thin slices of mature cheddar. Add a thin slice of mozzarella and then finely grate over a little parmesan. This will give you a great combination of creaminess and flavour. If you like a bit of bite then spread the bread with a little mustard first. This is a very rich sandwich and so great served with a green salad or even a pea soup.

Bacon and Cheese

When you want bacon in a panini then it is a good idea to cook it first. You can buy precooked crispy bacon pieces, but cooking bacon is so easy. You can use the panini press. Just pop it on the hot plate, put the lid down and cook for two minutes. While it is cooking, prepare your panini by putting some slices of cheddar cheese on it and then when the bacon is ready, put it in and cook the panini. Do not clean the panini press in between and any bacon juices left on the hot plate will soak in to your bread. This is also nice with tomato added or sun dried tomato spread on first. You may prefer some fresh cold tomatoes on the side.

Garlic Oil, Parma Ham and Cheese

Earlier on we explained how to make garlic oil. You will need to just brush a layer on to the bread. It is not necessary to have too much and the garlic flavour should easily come through. Spread some slice of the parma ham on top and then the cheese. An Italian cheese would seem appropriate for this dish and so mozzarella could be used but if you want something with a bit more flavour then a smoked cheddar could really liven it up.

Salami and Tomato

Salami can have a very strong flavour, especially if it is a really spiced version. It will tend to mask any other flavours that you add to it. This is why this dish just has slices of fresh tomato on the bread and then the salami. The tomato will add a freshness and moisture to the sandwich but the flavour will totally be that of the salami. You can add cheese as well, if you wish. Something creamy is best, like brie or goats cheese.

Tuna Melt

Many shops sell a tuna melt and it is a combination of tuna with cheese and a bechamel sauce. If you want an easy option, then you could just combine the tuna and some mozzarella but the sauce is very easy to make. You could make a lot and then keep in the fridge for a few days to use on lots of sandwiches or make just a small amount. For just the right amount to make one sandwich you would just need to melt a knob of butter in a small milk pan and add a teaspoon of plain flour. Then cover the bottom of the pan with milk and stir. If you tend to get lumps then use a whisk. Bring to he boil and simmer for a few minutes while stirring all the time. Pour on one side of bread, put tuna on top and then some small cubes of mozzarella.

Avocado, Tomato and Baby Spinach

This is a great panini for vegans. Use a ripe and soft avocado and a very ripe and juicy tomato. Slice the tomato and lay it on the bread. Then put slices of avocado on top and finely chop the baby spinach and sprinkle it on top. The avocado is in the middle because that is the place that gets the least heat and the avocado does not want to cook, but just warm through. The spinach will wilt, which will add a depth of flavour to the sandwich.

Breakfast Panini

You can put a great combination of breakfast items in a panini. You can make a vegetarian one with mushrooms, scrambled egg and tomato or something very meaty with sausages and bacon. It is important to cook some of the ingredients first though. The sausages need to be cooked and then sliced horizontally, so they fit well in the sandwich. The bacon can be cooked on the panini press before being put in the sandwich, as can the mushrooms. The eggs will need to be scrambled in advance too. With the eggs, make them quite runny, using milk or cream when you make them. If you just scramble eggs with butter and then recook them in the sandwich, they will go rubbery. It can really lift the panini to add some sweet tomato chutney.

Recommended combinations would be tomato chutney and mushroom, sausage, bacon and egg and bacon, egg and tomato. Experiment with it and see which will be your favourite.

Roasted Garlic, Red Pepper, Tomato and Mozzarella

Garlic goes very soft when it is roasted and so it can easily then be spread on panini. It is best roasted in some olive oil on a medium heat for about 30 minutes. You want it to be soft inside but not burnt so keep an eye on it. Press the cloves gently to see if they are soft. Once cooked make a slit in the skin and squash out the garlic purée. You will need about 3 cloves for one panini. Spread the garlic across one piece of bread.

The red pepper tastes better if it is roasted or grilled. You can grill it on the panini press. Cut it into thin strips and then put it in for just a minute. You want it brown but not burnt so you may want to cook it for a bit longer than this. Spread the red pepper over the garlic and then add slices of tomato. Use a lovely ripe tomato as this will have lots of flavour. Lastly sprinkle on some small pieces of mozzarella. These will add a creaminess to the dish and balance the tartness of the tomato.

Roasted Vegetables and Houmous

An earlier recipe explains how to make the roasted vegetables. Light and freshly tasting vegetables like peppers, aubergine and red onion work well here. Root vegetables would just get overpowered by the houmous. Once the vegetables have been cooked, the sandwich is very easy to put together. Just spread each piece of bread with houmous, spoon on some vegetables and then toast. This is another great vegan option, although you could replace the houmous with cheese if you like. Adding tomato, perhaps in the form of salsa or chutney can also really lift the dish.

Meatballs

If you want to put meatballs in a panini, then you will need to use small ones or cut them in half. They will need to be cooked first and it is probably best to grill them. You can always cook a batch in advance and keep them in the fridge. A tomato sauce works well with meatballs. Try cooking a very finely chopped onion with two cloves of garlic in some olive oil until see through and then pouring on a jar of passata. Then add two teaspoons of tomato paste and simmer for an hour. Then stir in some granulated sugar to taste, if necessary. Spread a spoonful of this on each side of the ciabatta bread and then sandwich the meatballs in between. You could even use some of the sauce for dipping if it needs more. You may like to add cheese to the panini as well.

Pesto, Tomato and Cheese

Pesto may seem like rather a general item to use as there are many different types. This recipe is best with olive pesto or basil. It balances the flavours of the cheese and tomato. Use a good tomato, ripe and juicy as you do not want the flavour to be lost among the strong pesto and cheese flavours. You do not want an extremely mature cheese but one that can hold its own so probably something that would be labelled as 'mature'.

Olives, Rocket and Tomato

There are a lot of strong flavours here but they work well together. Make sure you remove any stones from the olives before you use them. It is best to half the olives as well. As the olive and rocket flavours are strong it is good to have a nice sweet and juicy tomato. You may like to have some creamy cheese to set it all off as well.

Cheese and Marmite

Marmite and yeast extract has a great strong flavour and works very well with a cheese like Cheddar. Use plenty of cheese with just a thin spreading of Marmite, unless you love your Marmite strong!

Vegetable Chutney and Tomato

This is a great vegan option and it is also low calorie. Many paninis contain cheese and it can add a lot of additional calories, especially if you use a full fat cheese and lots of it. A panini does not need cheese, the chutney will make sure that it is not too dry, especially if you spread it generously on both slices of bread. Slice the tomato too, using a tasty, ripe one. This makes a great vegan option again. You can add avocado or rocket if you want to alter the flavour.

Ham and Djionnaise

Djionnaise is a combination of Djion mustard and mayonnaise. It is easy to make yourself by adding the mustard to some mayonnaise and means that you can make it as strong as you wish. However, you can also buy it ready made from supermarkets if you prefer. It is best to use a good quality ham or something smoked to give it good flavour, but it does work with any, if you have some that needs using up.

Falafel and Houmous

Falafels taste great with houmous and in a panini they are delicious. They warm through nicely. A bit of vegetable chutney can sweeten the sandwich a bit and some roasted vegetables can add interesting texture as well as flavour. You can even cook them wrapped up in a tortilla or pita bread to make them really authentic.

Chicken and Stuffing

Using left overs in a panini is a fantastic way to make an interesting sandwich and stop things going off in the back of the fridge. Meat such as chicken and pork works really well with stuffing in a panini although it will be dry so you will need to add a chutney, apple sauce or even some mozzarella to make it easier to eat.

Piccalilli, Ham and Cheese

Piccalilli has a very hot mustard flavour and so this is a great sandwich for anyone who loves that mustard heat. You can, of course have it just with ham or just with cheese, but having it with both provides a lovely creaminess to the flavour of the meat. A smoked or flavoursome ham is best or else it will be overwhelmed by the flavour of the piccalilli.

Pear and Stilton

Pear and Stilton are a classic combination and are delicious in a panini. It is best to cook the pear slightly first, so peel and cut it thinly. You can put it on the panini press until it browns and then place it in the sandwich with some Stilton crumbled over it. The cheese will melt all over the pear and you will get the string and slightly tart cheese flavour with the sweetness of the pear and the contrast in textures between the hard pear and oozing cheese.

Ham, Pineapple and Cheese

If you like a ham and pineapple pizza, then why not put that combination in your panini. Use a cooked ham for ease and then just lay it on the bread, put thinly sliced pineapple on top and then sprinkle with mozzarella. A creamy light flavoured cheese works best with this.

Roasted Vegetables, Olives and Tomato

This is a great vegan recipe. Spread the slice of bread with roasted vegetables and then slice some olives in half and sprinkle over the top. Lastly slice a big ripe and tasty tomato and lay these on top. As it heats through the flavours will mix and you will get sweet, tart and salty all in one delicious mouthful.

Avocado and Bacon

Spread one piece of bread with 1 tablespoon of salsa. Then put two cooked bacon rashers on top – you may like to slice these up. Put some grated cheese on top and then some sliced ripe avocado. You may also like to add some rocket as the flavour cuts through the richness of the cheese and avocado. An alternative to this is to use Stilton cheese and toasted pine nuts instead of grated cheese and you can leave out the salsa if you wish.

Cajun Crab

You will need about half a tin of crab meat for this. Mix it with a spoonful of mayonnaise, a dash of Worcestershire sauce, a sprinkle of Cajun seasoning and finely chopped red or green pepper. Sprinkle with parsley. Spread on one side of the panini and place on the lid. You can adjust the seasoning to taste or even leave it out altogether.

Crab Royale

This works very well in a panini instead of served in a crab shell. Just remove cooked crab from the shell and mix with a tablespoon of double cream, some fresh chopped parsley, a dash of Tabasco sauce and 1 tablespoon of grated parmesan cheese.

Creamy Fish

Mix 150g smoked fish with 150g cream cheese and the juice of a lemon with ½ tsp paprika. This makes enough for two sandwiches and so you can share it with someone else or it will keep in the fridge for the next day.

Chilli Chicken

Fry 50g of French beans in olive oil and fry with ½ tsp chilli flakes until cooked and then stir in 100ml double cream. Place it in the panini with slices of cooked chicken breast and sliced cherry tomatoes. You can replace the beans with other left over vegetables and will need to adjust the chilli to your taste.

Cheese and Mushroom

Grill a large mushroom and then slice it. Mix together 30g goats cheese with one tablespoon of chopped walnuts, one tablespoon of chopped parsley and some black pepper. Spread this on the panini base and then put the mushroom slices on top.

Christmas Dinner

Use slices of left over turkey and then spread cranberry sauce over it. Put some marscapone cheese on top and then some stuffing on top – sliced up. You could even put in any left over vegetables if you have them, like carrots or French beans or serve them on the side.

Sweet Panini Recipes

Chocolate Panini

If only chocolate will do then you can even have it inside your panini! You will need to chop the chocolate quite finely or use chocolate buttons or else it will not melt because the lumps will be too big. You could use a sweet bread for this, maybe a raisin loaf, although it may burn on the panini press if it is too sticky. Chocolate does work well with salt and butter so using brioche or croissants is very nice! Of course you can just use normal panini bread. Be careful with the quantity of chocolate because as it melts it may ooze out of the bread and burn on the panini press. You will just need a light sprinkling. Although chocolate on its own is delicious, you could also try adding marshmallows, chopped nuts, crushed ginger biscuits as well as cinnamon. You could also combine it with fruit such as slices of pear or banana.

Jam and Cream Cheese Panini

This makes a great snack or pudding and is very easy to prepare. Just spread one half of your bread with your favourite jam and the other with soft cheese. Mascapone is great for this but they are many similar alternatives that you may wish to try – just make sure that it is plain as one with added garlic or chives will be pretty disgusting! Bread choice can be important here too, walnut bread works well here, as would raisin loaf.

Cooked Apple Panini

The softness of cooked apple works really well in a panini. If it is very runny, then do not use too much as it will squash out of the panini and burn on the hot plate. Therefore spread it quite thinly and leave a good clear edge around the edge of the bread. This is great served sliced up and dipped in plain yoghurt.

Honey Panini

Honey has such a lovely flavour that it can work very well on its own in a panini. However, it is great if you combine it with other sweet things such as fresh fruit, bananas are particularly good as they go so soft.

Peanut Butter and Banana

This is a very simple panini to make but great if you need something which is salty and sweet. Just spread the panini with peanut butter and slice the banana thinly and lay it on top. You can add additional flavours if you like such as honey, demerera sugar or agave nectar. Using crunchy peanut butter adds texture as well.

Nutella and Banana

If you love the chocolatey and nutty flavour of Nutella then you will love it in a panini. Adding banana to it, gives it another dimension, a soft texture and the lovely sweetness. Make sure that you slice the banana thinly and place in between the slices of bread which should eat be coated with nutella.

Other Food to Cook on the Panini Press

Steak

Steak can easily be cooked on a panini press. The only thing to bear in mind is that it will cook twice as quickly as it would in a pan or on the grill because it is being cooked from both sides. Keep a close eye on it and make sure that it does not burn.

Bacon

As described earlier, it is easy to cook bacon on the panini press and it has the advantage of the fact that it keeps it flat so it cooks more evenly. It will take about two minutes to cook.

Mushrooms

Mushrooms should have any long stalks removed so that they can sit flatter on the hot plates. They may take quite a long time to cook, depending on how brown you like the outside. If you cook them for four minutes they will be soft and juicy inside but will have very little colouring to the outside. You may like to cook it for longer if you like the flavour that they get when they are browned. Keep a close check on them though as they could easily burn and will then not be very nice.

Vegetables

If you want to brown off vegetables such as onion, peppers or courgettes then this can be done easily too. Cut it to the size that you want it before you cook it and then check it every minute to see if it is cooked. Because it is in small pieces it should cook quite quickly. It is also great for cooking baby young vegetables such as asparagus tips, baby corn and things like that. It will cook them a little bit and give then a lovely char grilled flavour.

Toast

It is so easy to cook toast and it is much crunchier and more evenly cooked than from a conventional toaster. You can use all sorts of different type of bread.

Fruit

You can easily brown slices of apple or pear or even banana on the panini press before making in to a lovely sandwich or just eating them with some cream of ice cream.

Conclusion

I hope that you have enjoyed looking through this cook book. I have kept it all really simple but hope that the different combinations of flavours and textures will encourage you to not only try something new but to experiment for yourself and discover all sorts of wonderful new food combinations.

The panini press is so easy to use and saves a lot of time on washing up. It is easy to make nutritionally balanced meals which do not have to be packed full of calories and can be fun to make. They are a great fast food but can be a lot better for you than a take away or ready meal and can actually be quicker to cook.

Hopefully you will now be inspired to try something new and fun and even try out some new recipes on your friends and family. I hope that enjoy trying out some of the recipes and get lots of use out of your panini press.

7244608R00015

Printed in Great Britain
by Amazon.co.uk, Ltd.,
Marston Gate.